# The Faery Wife.
# Mary Ann Benbow

# The Burning of Bridget Cleary.

## Bridget Cleary

The policemen had been combing the green yards and fields of Ballyvadlea, Ireland, for a week when they finally found Bridget Cleary. The 26-year-old's body had been wedged beneath several inches of clay and a jumble of thorn bushes, but her corpse showed wounds caused by something much worse than branches: Her spine and lower limbs were so badly burned that parts of her skeleton were exposed. She was naked, except for a stocking and one gold earring, and her head was encased in a sack.

The judge would later describe the events leading up to Bridget's death as demonstrating "a degree of darkness in the mind, not just of one person, but of several—a moral darkness, even religious darkness." It was the end of the 19th century, not exactly the Middle Ages, but those involved in the end of Bridget's life had become convinced that she wasn't really herself—and that a supernatural creature had taken her place.

### GONE WITH THE FAIRIES

Bridget was the wife of a cooper named Michael Cleary, and the pair were regarded around town as a relatively happy couple. They shared their cottage, in a remote townland near Tipperary, with Bridget's father, Patrick Boland, and had no children. Michael was nine years Bridget's senior and earned a decent salary; she brought in some extra income by working as a seamstress and egg-seller. By all accounts, they were more prosperous than their neighbors, likely thanks to her resourcefulness. As a literate, independent, and fashionably dressed working woman, she was part of an emerging class in a rural society that had long been based in agriculture and the oral tradition.

It was also a society steeped in legends of the supernatural. Fairy belief, in particular, was pervasive in Irish rural societies at the time, and had long co existed with Christian doctrine. Children grew up hearing legends of the Little People from their earliest days, and learned how to appease them by leaving untasted food on the table, for example, or saying "bless them" whenever the fairies were mentioned. The fairies were blamed for everything that went wrong—lost items, spoiled milk, bad crops. As one County Sligo man interviewed at the start of the 20th century told an anthropologist, "Nothing is more certain than that there are fairies."

Bridget herself was known to be fascinated by the beings, and to take trips to the most fairy-ridden spots around town. She may have visited such a spot on Monday, March 4, 1895, when she went to deliver eggs to her father's cousin, Jack Dunne, near Kylenagranagh Hill. The area was home to a ringfort, an early medieval circular fortified settlement believed, in Irish folklore, to be a "fairy fort," and thus to be avoided at all costs. Yet Bridget often visited the fort, and she likely spent time there that Monday after delivering the eggs.

It was a cold morning, the mountains still covered in the snow that had fallen the previous day, and after the two- or three-mile walk Bridget couldn't seem to warm up once she got back home. She spent the following day in bed, shivering and complaining of "a raging pain in her head."

That Saturday, her father walked four miles in the heavy rain to ask the doctor to call on her. But the doctor wasn't able to visit until the following Wednesday, and by then her husband had also gone to summon him twice. They should have been reassured by the doctor's diagnoses—"nervous excitement and slight bronchitis"—but it wasn't this ailment that worried Michael. He was convinced that the bed-ridden woman in their cottage was "too fine," in his own words, to be his wife, and that she was "two inches taller" than the woman he had known. At some point, Michael had developed the belief that Bridget had been replaced by a fairy changeling as she passed near the fairy fort on Kylenagranagh Hill.

**"ARE YOU BRIDGET BOLAND?"**

It is likely that this idea was planted in Michael's head by his confidante, Jack Dunne. According to Irish historian Angela Bourke, who has researched the case extensively, the 55-year-old Dunne was a charismatic man rumored to have the power of divination. He was known in the area as a *seanchaí*, a sort of storyteller well-versed in fairy mythology.

On Wednesday afternoon, after the doctor's visit, a priest visited. He wasn't overly concerned about the illness, but decided to administer the last rites in case it worsened. The ceremony emphasized the fact that Michael could lose his wife, which distressed him even more. He talked to Dunne, who urged him to act immediately, or the "real" Bridget would be lost forever. "It is not your wife is there [sic]," the older man reminded him. "This is the eighth day, and you had a right to have gone to Ganey"—the local "fairy doctor"—"on the fifth day."

The cooper duly visited Ganey following morning. He came back with a mixture of herbs that needed to be boiled in "new milk," the nutrient-rich first milk produced by a cow after calving.

That night, Michael forced the bitter concoction down Bridget's throat while Dunne and three male cousins pinned her down in bed. Relatives outside the house heard someone—likely Michael—shouting, "Take it, you witch, or I'll kill you!" The men threw urine at her and shook her, yelling, "Away with you; come home Bridget Boland, in the name of God!" Other relatives and neighbors came and went, witnessing her ordeal and hearing her screams, but were too scared to intervene. Michael asked his wife to answer her name three times: "Are you Bridget Boland, wife of Michael Cleary, in the name of God?" The men then brought her to the fireplace and held her over the grate—ordeals by fire were known to drive out the fairies—while they repeated the questioning.

By midnight Thursday night, the ritual seemed to be completed. Bridget was "wild and deranged," according to her cousin Johanna, but her husband seemed satisfied, and her relatives thought there had been some sort of catharsis. The following morning, at Michael's request, the priest said mass in Bridget's bedroom in order to banish the "evil spirits" that were left in the house.

## "IT IS NOT BRIDGET I AM BURNING."

On Friday, March 15, for the first time in 11 days, Bridget got out of bed and dressed in her usual, fashionable clothes "to give her courage when she would go among the people," as Johanna later told the magistrates. Several family members had joined them in their cottage for tea later in the day when an argument erupted. Bridget had asked for some milk, which had rekindled Michael's suspicions; fairies are known in folklore to yearn for fresh milk.

Bridget was probably exhausted, and she didn't want to be questioned any more. "Your mother used to go with the fairies and that is why you think I am going with them," she told her husband. Michael was furious. He demanded that she eat three pieces of bread and jam—perhaps to reinforce his control over her—asking her to say her name again. She answered twice and ate two of the three pieces, but when she hesitated for a moment with the third, her husband flung her on the ground and threatened her: "If you won't take it, down you will go."

Michael jabbed his knee into her chest, forcing the bread and jam down Bridget's throat. He began tearing off her clothes, leaving only her chemise, then grabbed a hot stick from the fire and held it close to her mouth. He struck her head against the floor, then set her chemise alight. Within a few minutes, he had also poured paraffin lamp oil over her, encouraging the flames.

As her body was burning, Michael said in front of shocked relatives: "She's not my wife. She's an old deceiver sent in place of my wife." Relatives yelled at Michael to put out the flames, but Bridget "blazed up all in a minute," according to their later testimony. They huddled in fear in a nearby bedroom, the flames soon barricading their way.

Once the flames had died down, Michael wrapped her body in a sheet and shoved it in an old bag. Then he left the house, locking Bridget's relatives inside with the corpse. They waited for about an hour, praying. When Michael returned, he was wielding a knife and threatened to kill Bridget's cousin Patrick Kennedy if he didn't help him bury Bridget's body. "Come on out here now," he shouted. "I have the hole nearly made." The two men carried the body to a boggy area about a quarter-mile uphill from the cottage, and buried it in a shallow hole. Back in the cottage, Michael made the rest of the family swear they wouldn't tell the authorities.

## ON A WHITE HORSE

The following morning, an agitated Michael arrived at Drangan church with Dunne. Dunne wanted Michael to speak to a priest, but when the priest saw him kneeling in front of the altar—weeping, tearing his hair, and asking to go to confession—he thought he wasn't fit to receive the sacrament. He spoke to Dunne instead, who hadn't been at the cottage at the time of Bridget's death, but told the priest that Michael had claimed to have burned his wife the previous night. "I've been asking them all morning to take her up and give her a Christian burial," Dunne added. Bewildered, thinking them both insane, the church minister reported their conversation to a police sergeant.

For the next few days, the police searched for Bridget and questioned her friends and relatives. Even though Michael spoke about emigrating or committing suicide to escape the law, he still hoped his "real wife" would come back: For three consecutive nights starting the day after visiting the priest, he waited at the ringfort on Kylenagranagh Hill, where he believed she would appear, galloping on a white horse. He said he would only have to cut the ropes that bound her to the animal so she would be his forever.

On Wednesday, March 20, the Royal Irish Constables issued arrest warrants for eight people from Bridget's circle, as well as Denis Ganey, the "fairy doctor." Two days later, police found Bridget's body. The prisoners were brought before the magistrates on March 25, ushered in by the angry screams of a crowd who had learned of the case through extensive press coverage. On July 5, 1895, after a two-day trial, Michael was found guilty of manslaughter and imprisoned, along with Jack Dunne, Patrick Boland, and four of Bridget's cousins, including Patrick Kennedy. The judge ruled out a verdict of murder, explaining they all had acted out of genuine belief.

Michael was released in 1910, after which he boarded ship for Montreal. Dunne served a three-year prison sentence before returning to the area, where he kept working as a laborer. "God knows I would never do it but for Jack Dunne," Michael had reportedly said not long after burning Bridget. "It was he who told me my wife was a fairy."

## ILLNESS—OR INFIDELITY?

During her illness, Bridget was visited by her aunt, Mary Kennedy, and told her, "He [Michael]'s making a fairy of me now. He thought to burn me about three months ago." Her words suggest this wasn't the first crisis of its kind.

Although we can only speculate about the couple's disagreements, there were rumors in Ballyvadlea that Bridget had a lover. Contemporary newspapers reported Michael saying his wife "used to be meeting an egg-man on the low road" [sic], but the rumors pointed to young caretaker William Simpson, who had visited the Clearys' cottage with his wife the night before Bridget's death. In his court testimony, Simpson explained he had arrived as the four men were restraining Bridget, and he had asked them to leave her alone.

Although Michael and the other people involved in the killing were never formally psychiatrically assessed, a 2006 from the *Irish Journal of Medical Science* suggested that Michael may have been suffering from a psychotic state known as Capgras syndrome, which involves the belief that a person has been replaced by an impostor. The authors suggest Michael "may have developed a brief psychotic episode" as he struggled to deal with his wife's illness, sleep deprivation, and the recent death of his father—news of which had reached him in the middle of his attempted "cure" on Thursday night. In Capgras syndrome, the socio-cultural context of the sufferer determines the nature of the impostor, which can be another person or even a supernatural being, such as an alien or a fairy changeling.

In her discussion of the supernatural beliefs related to the case, Bourke notes that the message of fairy legends is that "the unexpected may be guarded against by careful observance of society's rules." Bridget Cleary was ambitious, independent, and childless; a modern woman. She didn't conform to the patriarchal norm, which may have made her appear, to some in her life, as closer to the fairy realm than to their own.

Even today in Tipperary, her story hasn't been entirely forgotten. The local children have a nursery rhyme that runs: "Are you a witch or are you a fairy, / Or are you the wife of Michael Cleary?"

There aren't many murders in Irish history as famous as that of the burning of Bridget Cleary. There's even a chilling children's rhyme that girls jump rope to – "Are you a witch or are you a fairy? Are you the wife of Michael Cleary"?

Twelve years into her marriage to Michael Cleary, Bridget Cleary got sick. She was a childfree, 26-year-old dressmaker with her own egg business, and February had been a particularly cold month – the coldest on record at the time in the United Kingdom, in fact. On Monday, March 4, Bridget went out to deliver her eggs to customers. It another bitterly cold day, though sunny, and it had snowed the previous day. According to witnesses, she waited two hours for her father's cousin, Jack Dunne, but he never returned. Chilled, she went back home, and tried to warm herself by the fire. She went to bed still cold that night, and woke the next day complaining of a headache, shivering, and feverish. She stayed in bed for most of that week.

 The records we have about the events of the next ten days come from court testimonies. Eleven people were arrested in connection to Bridget's death, including her cousin, Johanna Burke. Burke turned Queen's witness in exchange for immunity, and provided the main thread of the story as it has since been told. How much Burke played up or downplayed certain elements to protect herself, or her brothers – all three of whom had been arrested as well – we simply cannot know. Though Bridget's older cousin, Johanna Burke lived a very different life from Bridget. She had at least four children in 1895, lived in one of the dilapidated daub and wattle homes. She had neither the economic independence nor freedom of a childless marriage that Bridget had. It is entirely conceivable that her role in Bridget's death was very different from the master narrative she wove for the magistrate and courts. The story she told suggested that Jack Dunne – Bridget's father's cousin, known throughout Tipperary as an accomplished storyteller well versed in fairy lore – was the prime instigator in the fairy tales about Bridget Cleary.

According to the court records, Patrick Boland walked the nearly nine miles from Ballyvadlea to Fethard to fetch the local doctor on Saturday, March 9. Bridget had been in bed sick since Tuesday. The doc still hadn't shown up by Monday, March 11. Michael Cleary made the trip to Fethard this time, to summon the doctor. Still, the doctor did not show up. Michael walked again to Fethard on Wednesday, demanding that the doctor see his wife. While he was out, he stopped at Jack Dunne's and asked him to visit Bridget. Michael also stopped to ask Bridget's aunt, Johanna Burke's mother, Mary Kennedy, to visit when she could. Both stopped in that day, as well as Johannah Burke. The priest also stopped in, and upon seeing Bridget's condition, he administered the last rites – just in case. Bridget's cousin, aunt, and father's cousin, Jack Dunne, were all still there when the doctor finally came. He told them that she had a touch of bronchitis, and left Michael with a vial of medicine.

In his statement, Michael Cleary insisted that the doctor was drunk when he came to the house. Though none of the other witnesses could attest to that, later the doctor was dismissed from his parish position for chronic drunkenness, so it seems as likely as not. But Michael Cleary had perhaps already made up his mind about his wife, for on the second trip out to summon the doctor, he apparently stopped at a local fairy doctor and procured some "herbs" to administer to his ailing wife. None of the witnesses could say whether he ever gave Bridget any of the doctor's medicine, but all were present when he gave her his own cure.

According to Johanna's testimony, Bridget was particularly agitated on Wednesday. She whispered to her cousin that she had a pain in her head, and that "Michael Cleary was making a fairy of her, and that he had tried to burn her three months ago."[1] Johanna, her mother Mary Kennedy, and Jack Dunne stayed at the Cleary's until late – possibly even staying the night entirely. On Thursday, March 14, Michael Cleary again ventured out into the unseasonably cold March whether to seek the advice of fairy herbalist Denis Ganey. Ganey would ultimately be arrested in connection with Bridget's death, though he never visited the house himself. Jack Dunne reportedly insisted that Ganey be consulted – that, in fact, the advice of the parish doctor was pointless, because Bridget's case was one of fairy mischief.

 So when Michael returned, he had the instructions for turning the herbs he'd obtained into a 'cure.' Quite a few of Bridget's relatives were in the house when Michael returned, as well as their neighbor, William Simpson, and his wife. Bridget's cousins – two of Mary Kennedy's sons Patrick and James – showed up around 9pm that night with bad news: Michael's father had passed away, and they were planning to attend the wake. For Jack Dunne, the bad news reaffirmed the fairy's role in Bridget's illness – according to lore, the fairies used tragedies to distract watchful family members from noticing the wasting of their changeling loved one. Cleary said to Dunne, "I have something here that will make her all right." And Dunne replied, "Three days ago you had a right to be beyond with Ganey, for the doctor had nothing to do with her. It is not your wife is there. You will have enough to do to bring her back. This is the eighth day."

According to Dunne, Michael Cleary locked the door, and said "'I think then, it is time to give her this.' He had [the 'cure' – herbs boiled in new milk -] in a pint, which he held against his breast; the four of us caught her and I had her by the neck; it was very hard on her to take it; Cleary told me that after taking that she should be brought to the fire; so we brought her to the fire; we raised her over it, but did not burn her; I thought it belonged to the cure; he told me it belonged to the cure."

When Johanna Burke arrived that evening, just before 10pm, she was met on the road to the house by the Cleary's neighbors, the Simpsons. They found the front door locked, and shouts and screams from inside. Someone yelled "Take that, you witch, or I'll kill you." Eventually, Michael opened the door. Patrick Boland – Bridget's father – was in the kitchen, but everyone else was in the bedroom. Bridget was in her undergarments on the bed, and Jack Dunne was sitting beside her, holding her ears to keep her head still. Bridget's cousins James and Patrick were holding her arms, and William Kennedy lay across her legs. Mary Kennedy, Bridget's aunt, watched from the door of the bedroom. Bridget was struggling against the men, and against the bitter mixture that Michael was trying to spoon into her mouth. Over and over, Michael and Jack asked her if she was Bridget Cleary, if she was Patrick Boland's daughter and Michael Cleary's wife. Over and over, she said yes. Over the next few hours, the men carried her struggling and feverish body to the kitchen, and held her over the low but undeniably warm fire, before carrying her back to the bedroom and forcing more of the mixture down her throat. They shouted at her, demanding that she affirm her identity again and again. They used a hot poker, held against her face, to force her to open her mouth and swallow. They threw liquids on her – possibly water and wine, but more likely urine. Three times they poured the 'medicine' into her mouth and made her swallow it. Repeatedly they carried her over to the fire, holding her over it. As the *Southern Star* reported in 1895, "When they held her over the fire she had only her night-dress and chemise on. They repeated the questions, and she replied–'I am Bridget Boland, daughter of Pat Boland, and wife of Michael Cleary, in the name of God.'" Three times appeared to be the charm. Johanna Burke testified that, while Bridget was still noticeably agitated – understandably – the men seemed calmer. The power of three satisfied them. She took three doses, and she answered their demands as they held her over the fire. Michael seemed, that evening, surrounded by her family and their neighbors, to accept that she was Bridget Cleary. They put her back in her bed, and her cousin Johanna and her aunt Mary Kennedy cleaned her up, put her in a new nightgown. She was broken, defeated, put in her place by the men in her life.

Once she was clothed again, the men returned to the bedroom, standing around the bed, and asked her to identify each of them. She complied. Satisfied, they all spoke consolingly to her, telling her all would be well, she was safe now. All seemed well. Bridget's male cousins and her father left to go to Michael Cleary's father's wake. The Simpsons went home. Johanna Burke, her mother Mary Kennedy, and Michael stayed up late talking in the kitchen, until Michael left early the next morning to fetch the priest. He requested that the priest administer a Mass to Bridget that morning, for she'd had quite a trying night, and could use the spiritual support.

Father Ryan rode to the Cleary's and said the Mass. After the priest left, Johanna Bourke told the courts that there was an argument about a milk delivery. Bourke provided the Clearys with their milk – including the new milk (which is the first milk after a cow gives birth) – that Michael forced down his wife's throat the night before. As the *Southern Star* reported, Johanna testified that "Bridget asked her husband if I had been paid for the milk, and he said yes. I took the shilling out of my pocket, and showed it to her. She took it in her hand, and put it under the bed-clothes, and gave it back to me."

This was the straw, evidently, to break the camel's back. In rural Ireland, women who rubbed a coin on their inner thigh or – more scandalously – their vulva did so to temporarily give the holder of that coin bad luck. The only witness to this action, however, was Johanna Burke – so, again, we can't say whether it happened or not, and to that end, whether the subsequent argument and ultimate murder can be connected to that alleged curse. But that's the way Johanna Burke told the story. As historian Angela Bourke notes in *The Burning of Bridget Cleary* though, even if she did rub the coin on her thigh, it needn't have had malicious intent. "It could have been almost automatic, as when some Catholics make the sign of the cross on their bodies." But unlike an acceptable Catholic motion, this would have been associated with the "piseogery" that Bridget's family had shaken, scalded, and choked out of her the night before. Bridget dressed fully for the first time in over a week. She sat in the kitchen by the fire. Life seemed to have returned to normal. Friends and family circulated in and out of the house for the remainder of the day, laughing and joking and relaxing. As Angela Bourke notes, even the role of Jack Dunne, the purveyor of the fairy tales that effectively punished Bridget for being too independent, too wealthy, too childless in a world that resented women guilty of any of those crimes, was over. He'd done his job, and had gone home. It seemed, to Johanna Burke, to the Kennedy boys and their mother, to Patrick Boland, that it was over.

But, as we know, it was not. According to Johanna Burke, "her husband spoke to her about rubbing the shilling to her leg. She got angry, and said there were no "pishogues" about her. There was talk about fairies, and Bridget Cleary said to her husband, 'Your mother used to go to the fairies, and that is the reason you think I am going to them.' He asked her, 'Did my mother tell you that?' and she replied, 'She did; she gave two nights to them.' I made the tea, and offered Bridget Cleary a cup of it. Her husband got three bits of bread and jam, and said she should eat them before she took a sip. He asked her three times, "Are you Bridget Cleary, my wife, in the name of God?" She answered twice, and ate two pieces of the bread and jam. When she didn't answer the third time he forced her to eat the third piece of bread, saying, 'Eat it, or down you'll go.'"

 Down she went. Johanna Burke went on to describe the grisly scene. "He flung her on the ground, put his knee on her chest, caught her by the throat and forced the bit of bread and jam into her mouth, saying, "Swallow it; is it down?–is it down?" I called out to him, "Mike, Mike, don't you see 'tis Bridgie is in it," meaning that it was Bridget Cleary his wife who was there, and not a fairy. He suspected she was a fairy and not his wife at all. He stripped his wife's clothes off except the chemise, and got a blazing stick out of the fire. She was lying on the floor and he put the red stump across her mouth. My brothers and I said we would smash the door and go for the peelers [the police], but Cleary repeated that the door would not be opened and no one would leave the house until his wife came back. When he put the lighting stick near her mouth he called on her to answer her name three times. He said he would burn her if she didn't answer. She answered him, but the answer didn't satisfy him, and he got a tin of lamp oil and poured it over her . In a few minutes I saw her in a blaze. The house was filled with the fumes of the oil and burning. When I looked down in the kitchen I saw the remains of Bridget Cleary on a sheet."

Bridget Cleary wasn't the only Irish woman to be murdered by her husband in 19th century Ireland. The *Freeman's Journal* reported on a wife murder trial in Dublin not two months after Bridget Cleary's death. 34-year-old Bridget Bolton was killed by her husband, William, in their home on 15 May, 1895. The coroner hypothesized that her neck was snapped, resulting in instantaneous death. Her body also had lacerations, one on the inside of a breast – possibly caused by a kick, but more likely by some instrument – and on her temple. As their daughter, Ellen, aged 11, testified, the two were "always quarrelling," and "her father was in the habit of beating her [mother]," and that her mother "drank heavily occasionally," but her father "constantly drank." William Bolton was punished three times for ill-treating Mrs. Bolton, and he was – according to little Ellen – "in the habit of accusing [Ellen's] mother of being dishonest." Ellen also told the court that her father had long since stopped supporting her and her mother. Even when they were separated, Mrs. Bolton gave her husband food and supported his drunken useless ass. The previous Christmas, Ellen witnessed her father grab her mother, twisted her arm and then broke it across his knee. That was the most recent assault he'd been punished for – he got two months imprisonment, though Mrs. Bolton got a month herself, because she refused to prosecute her abuser.

Domestic violence was all too common in 19th century Ireland. As Diane Urquart "surveys of Irish national and regional papers in the 1870s reveal weekly cases of wife-beating in the magistrates' courts, and criminal records from 1853 to 1920 include over 1000 appeals from Irishmen convicted of domestic violence." Wife-beating in Ireland was widespread and brutal. Wife murder was a more likely result than women being granted a divorce. Most familiar with modern Irish history are probably aware that divorce was illegal in the 26 counties (the Irish Free State from 1922-1949, and the Republic of Ireland thereafter) until a referendum on the constitution was passed in 1995. But prior to Irish independence, it was still difficult for women to secure divorces and leave bad marriages. Though divorce was technically legal, Ireland did not benefit from the 1857 Divorce and Matrimonial Clause, which moved most United Kingdom divorce proceedings from a parliamentary appeal to the standard court system. It allowed women to sue for the divorce when there was evidence of adultery and desertion for at least two years.

Certainly obtaining a divorce, even through the court system, was no walk in the park for a British woman, and divorce proceedings were often the hottest news in the gossip rags, airing the most intimate of dirty laundry of middling and upper class couples for all to read. Still, while women in the rest of the United Kingdom had at least some recourse for getting out of bad marriages, the new law was not applied to overwhelmingly Catholic Ireland. While the Catholic hierarchy did not officially oppose the new legislation, British lawmakers apparently deemed the potential opposition from the emancipated Catholics too high to try and apply the law to Ireland. Thus at the end of the 19th century, divorce requests continued to be submitted to the Irish parliament for consideration.

Sarah: Parliamentary granted divorces usually required three separate steps: usually involved three separate legal suits: divorce a mensa et thoro to allow separation so that the parties could live apart but could not remarry; a civil action brought by a husband to claim damages from his wife's lover in the common law courts, popularly known as crim. con., — essentially adultery — and a private act of parliament to grant divorce *a vinculo matrimonii*.[10] These suits were immensely expensive, costing between 200 and 5000 pounds, and certainly out of the realm of possibility for women like Bridget Bolton or Bridget Cleary.

And, significantly, the parliamentary process was particularly biased in favor of men. Women were most likely to lose custody of their children, have their character slandered in public, and, because all of their property became their husband's upon marriage, lose virtually everything, The very first divorce case granted to an Irish woman was in 1886, approved by Westminster, on the grounds of domestic abuse.[11] This set a precedent in the waning years of the 19th century, but the barriers to the average Irish woman continued to be insurmountable. Most had to stay with their abusive husbands, were economically and socially bound into unhappy and painful marriages. The system was sympathetic to wife-beating husbands. They were given passes when they could articulate how they were "correcting" their wives." And women who stayed with these husbands were credited with trying to make their marriage work. Some paid the ultimate price.

And some husbands even got away with wife murder. Such was the case of William Bolton, despite evidence given by his daughter that there was a history of violence, that she had other marks on her body indicating an altercation, and that he was in the house when she fell – and ran out of the

house shortly thereafter. The other witnesses, including other borders in the slum tenement where the Boltons were living, could not say whether her fall, which broke her neck, was an accident or if he pushed her down the stairs, and so the jury came back to say that there was not enough evidence to indict him. Michael Cleary did not have the benefit of no witnesses to his murder. Bridget's cousins, father, and neighbor were all in the house watching him kill her. And yet Michael Cleary was the only husband in 19th century Ireland to get a more lenient sentence based on his professed belief that the woman he killed was not his wife, but a changeling.

It'd be easy to dismiss Michael Cleary as crazy. By modern standards, perhaps he would have been diagnosed with temporary insanity under the circumstances. All accounts suggest he had been walking all over the Tipperary countryside, fetching the parish doctor, the priest, and family members to look in on his wife. He hadn't slept much in the week or so before he doused his wife in lamp oil. He listened to the assurances of local wisemen – fairy men Jack Dunne and Denis Ganey – that the symptoms were that of someone fairy touched. Maybe he was convinced, or convinced himself, that his wife was a changeling, and per fairy lore, the final cure was fire. Maybe he truly believed enough in fairies to see one in his sick wife.

One of the most interesting elements of the case, though, isn't just this question of Michael Cleary, his crime, and his fairy defense. Rather, this case highlights the division of rural and urban Ireland and the rest of the United Kingdom. Michael Cleary's case rests on a belief – by the jurors, judge, and police – that the people of Tipperary believed in fairies. There is ample evidence, in the case presented, in earlier cases, and in the oral histories taken of Ireland after the Famine, to suggest that in most places in rural Ireland, some semblance of belief in the fae persisted throughout the 19th and early 20th century, despite or at least alongside Catholicism's revival and restructuring at the same time. But most likely, as Angela Bourke evidences in *The Burning of Bridget Cleary*, that 'belief' was very limited. In most cases, fairy tales functioned as morality tales, stories to define social norms and warn those who were transgressing. Instead of the ardently superstitious, Bourke argues, rural Ireland was more a mix of convenient belief in the fae — particularly when tragedy struck. An illness that suddenly took an infant or child could be blamed on fairies planting a changeling. Locals spoke of women and teen girls taken into the fairy forts that dotted Ireland's landscape, to live among the fairies – when in reality they fled to London or Dublin, seeking any life other than that of domestic violence and impoverishment in rural Ireland.

Lore lived on in Ireland largely, until the Gaelic Revival, because of the fairy women and fairy men – wise, older, usually disabled individuals who prescribed herbal cures, told the stories of the Ireland's rich mythological past, and provided guidance to those dealing with the diseases and symptoms lore associated with fairy interference. Bridget Cleary's cousin, Jack Dunne, who helped Michael Cleary administer the herbs boiled in new milk to Bridget, was one such individual. Though not the fairy man that Cleary went to for herbs – that was Denis Ganey – Dunne was a respected orator, known for his storytelling skill, and made a living at that. These individuals weren't the sole authorities in Victorian Ireland. The agents of Irish modernity were increasingly visible in all corners of the island. University-trained doctors, the Royal Irish Constabulary – a modern police force created in 1822 to surveil the provinces of Ireland – and, of course, the expanding legion of Catholic priests throughout Ireland. These various entities worked in concert and opposition to control and administer to the people of rural Ireland, to replace and preserve the heritage of fae and superstition.

Charles Dickens and countless other scholars of the Victorian period argued that literacy and Victorian literature killed the superstitious belief in fairies in the United Kingdom. Generally the rise of print media is associated with a 'modernisation' of the middling and educated Anglophone world. But, as Caroline Sumpter evidences, literacy and accessible printed materials actually served to reaffirm and spread fairy lore. Lady Augusta Gregory, WB Yeats, Lady Wilde, and, in the 1930s, the Folklore Commission of the Free State of Ireland – among others – collected the mythologies, legends, and fairy tales of Celtic Ireland. They preserved those stories in a world otherwise designed to wipe out pagan superstition. They published the collected lore in journals, poetry collections, books, children's magazines, and shillings monthlies, consumed extensively by the increasingly literate public.[12]

 This obviously isn't to suggest that reading about fairies in children's books means that adults grow up to believe their sick wives are changelings.

That's not the correlation that Sumpter is making, and it's not the correlation we're making. Instead, what is interesting is that the facilitators of the Gaelic Revival, the people who preserved the cultural heritage of fairy lore, were upper-class, educated, largely urban elite Victorian men and women. They were not remotely like the people they interviewed to collect those stories, and in their romantic narratives of the quaint Celtic fringe folk, they propagated a particular vision of rural Ireland: illiterate, superstitious, backwards, barbarians. Michael Cleary's heinous crime, and his insistence that he did so because he believed she was a fairy, was further evidence for the British newspaper-reading public that the Irish were unfit to rule themselves. For the jury that accepted Cleary's tale of changelings and ringforts, *of course* this country bumpkin believed his wife was a fairy. That was just par for the course.

Take Michael J. McCarthy, a Trinity-educated Irish lawyer known mostly for his anti-papism writings in an increasingly Catholic Ireland. In 1901 McCarthy wrote, "I sincerely pity all the people connected with these tragedies, but I pity still more intensely the many peasants who border upon, if they do not firmly entertain, the beliefs expressed in these … cases. This latter feeling is the gadfly which urges me on, as it urged Socrates of old, to do what little I can to crush out those remnants of savagery which should by this time be as extinct as the snakes in this so-called "Island of Saints.""

But this was not the backwards group of bumpkins one might've assumed from the reports coming out of Ireland. Johanna Burke testified that she told Bridget she didn't believe in fairies, and certainly didn't believe Bridget was a changeling. Michael Cleary was a literate craftsman. He apprenticed as a cooper in Clonmel, the 'big city' (relatively speaking), about 16 miles from Bridget's hometown of Ballyvadlea in County Tipperary. He met Bridget there when he was working, and she was apprenticing in a dressmaker's shop. And Bridget spent four years in Clonmel learning her craft, and bought a sewing machine of her own to take back to Ballyvadlea. Both Bridget and Michael would've been National school educated, Bridget perhaps all the way to the official leaving age of 14, after which she took up her apprenticeship.

They married in the mid-1880s, and for the first four years of their union, she lived in Ballyvadlea with her ailing mother and elderly father, and he lived in Clonmel, visiting her on the weekends. After her mother passed away, Bridget, Michael, and Bridget's father, Patrick Boland, applied for and were granted tenantship of the only new-build laborers cottage in Ballyvadlea. Michael moved in, and started making barrels for the local dairies. This took some smart finagling – these government-subsidized housing projects were to be reserved for farm labourers, and only Bridget's elderly father qualified. They used his technical designation to secure the finest home in Ballyvadlea. As a pair, Bridget and Michael Cleary were quite well-off, compared to their neighbors and family members. Bridget's dressmaking income and egg sales set her starkly above the other women in her community, including her cousin, Johanna Burke, the Queen's witness in the case against Michael Cleary.

It seems unlikely that an educated, skilled, smart man like Michael Cleary bought into fairy lore. Angela Bourke suggests that his disheveled mental state – worry over his ailing wife and the feverish things she was saying, lack of sleep and adequate food intake, and walking all over Tipperary in search of help for Bridget – was exploited by resentful and superstitious family members. It was Jack Dunne who suggested that a fairy cure was needed, and not to heed the doctor. The doctor's drunkenness probably didn't help to inspire confidence. But the Cleary's relative prosperity in a deeply impoverished region certainly didn't help their situation. And there's also the possibility of some underlying currents of resentment – after all, Bridget wasn't merely rising above her own kin. Her economic ventures and the couple's childlessness, while freeing economically, were likely a source of strain, possibly even resentment, between the two. Undoubtedly Michael blamed his wife for the failure to conceive a child. None or any of these symptoms alone might be cause for wife murder; but certainly the convergence of these conditions created a very dangerous situation for Bridget Cleary.

Bridget Cleary's story is also unique in that, while she wasn't the only suspected fairy murdered in nineteenth-century Ireland, she was the only adult. Stories about children being taken by the fairies – babies dying suddenly of wasting sicknesses, or children murdered by terrified parents – were mental leaps that allowed people to exist in a world of high infant mortality, poverty, and sickness. But Bridget was a grown woman. The continuous accusation that she was a changeling is the strangest and most suspicious element of the case.

Sir William Wilde — Oscar's father — was a doctor who studied both fairy folklore and catalogued the illnesses of his patients in the Irish countryside. The 19th century newspapers are also peppered with stories of children "fairy struck" — the *Morning Post* reported in 1836 that "Ann Roche, an old woman of very advanced age, was indicted for the murder of Michael Leahy, a young child, by drowning him in the Flesk. This case...turned out to be a homicide committed under the delusion of the grossest superstition. The child, though four years old, could neither stand, walk, nor speak—it was thought to be fairy struck..."

: Disturbing, deeply sad, and complicated in their own right, the murder of children who were suspected of being changelings is consistent with a fairly standard fairy lore: changelings almost universally took the place of children. And there are no other cases of adults being murdered for being a suspected changeling. As we've already suggested, fairy tales were by and large allegorical, or morality tales, not hard and fast facts. Angela Bourke has some really fascinating conclusions about this case, which we won't recount here. I definitely recommend you pick up a copy of her book, which is an excellent study of rural 19th century Ireland. I assigned it to my undergrads regularly, it's really a great read, and pulls together so much of what makes Irish history fascinating — threads gendered political, social, economic, and religious clash that converge in the horrific murder of an independent woman.

What is most disturbing to me is the bystander element of this story. Johanna Burke was not the only one present as Michael Cleary murdered his wife. According to the court testimonies, Patrick and James Kennedy were napping in Bridget's father's room – not far from the commotion in the kitchen by any means, if they were even really sleeping there – and Mary Kennedy was sleeping in the Cleary's bed. But Patrick Boland, Johanna Burke, and William Kennedy were all in the kitchen when Michael attacked his wife for the final time. Johanna says she cried out, telling him to stop – but made no move to stop him. William, a strapping and tall 21-year-old man, did nothing to pull the violent man off of his cousin.

Sarah: Perhaps they were stunned by the outburst. Perhaps they, in some deeper part of their subconscious, believed she was a fairy. Perhaps they wished her ill. Everyone behaved so bizarrely, unfeelingly, on that terrible Friday night. When Michael stood over his wife's burned body, he told the (reportedly) shocked family members present that it was done now, and Bridget would come to the local fairy fort on a white horse, and that they had to be there to free her from the fairies with an iron knife. Patrick Kennedy helped Michael Cleary bury his wife in a shallow grave, wearing nothing but a sack over her head and her black stockings. He convinced a bewildered William Kennedy to go with him that very night to wait outside the ringfort for three nights. Surely, he told them, she'd appear by the end of three nights.

Of course, she did not appear. She was dead, first shoved hastily into an 18 inch hole, and later buried quietly by the RIC in Clonen, under the cover of darkness on Wednesday March 27, a charred corpse. In early investigations, people like Johanna Burke swore to the local constables that Bridget got up and walked out of the house when she was put to the fire. Most perpetuated Cleary's delusion / cover story. As early as Saturday the 16th there were rumors of foul play regarding Bridget's disappearance. William Simpson went to the police on Monday, March 18, and when the constables went for a second round of questions, Johanna Burke changed her tune, and gave a new statement.

On March 21st, those connected to the murder were arrested. When the Royal Irish Constabulary found her body on March 22, they'd already arrested 11 people – Johanna Burke; her mother, Mary Kennedy; her sons, William, Patrick, Michael, and James Kennedy; Bridget's father, Patrick Boland; Jack Dunne; the herb doctor, Denis Ganey; a 16-year-old boy who'd been present at the milk fiasco; and, of course, Michael Cleary. Ganey was soon released, when it was clear he had no direct involvement in the murder. Johanna Burke, as we've said, turned Queen's witness and was granted immunity from prosecution.

The jury, after three days of testimonies and nearly a month of evidence-collecting by the RIC, and just 40 minutes of deliberation, returned with guilty verdicts for all nine remaining prisoners. They strongly recommended Patrick Boland, Michael Kennedy, and Mary Kennedy to mercy. They found Patrick Kennedy most guilty, besides Michael Cleary, for his role in the disposal of the body – he got 5 years imprisonment. Jack Dunne got 3 years, less than the 5 the judge thought he deserved on account of his age. William and James Kennedy got 18 months. Patrick Boland and Michael Kennedy got 6 months imprisonment, and Mary Kennedy got none.

About Michael Cleary, the judge delivered quite a pronouncement. "The short of the matter was that he burned his wife alive…[I do] not know that these medicines the prisoner procured, or those herbs were really intended for the cure," but the judge could also not say whether or not Michael Cleary was mad, because there hadn't been a lengthy inquest into that line of thought. All the same, the judge continued, "the fact that the prisoner inflicted upon the woman whom he swore before the altar to cherish and protect–that he took her life away [in what was] generally regarded the most cruel and painful of human afflictions, by burning her alive. Dead she was not at the time he threw the paraffin oil on her, and his wicked hand sent her to another world in the very prime of her life–a young woman who confessed to him her affections and her life and he most wantonly and most cruelly and most wretchedly betrayed her."

All the same, the judge found himself doubting the clarity of the case enough that he stopped short of the extreme sentence. He did not doubt Michael Cleary's guilt, but he did doubt Cleary's sanity in the case. And so he remanded Cleary to 20 years penal servitude. According to the *Irish Examiner*, during the delivery of the sentence, "the prisoner wept bitterly.

Ireland in the 1890s was a country in turmoil. Along with a population still devastated by the Great Famine just a few decades previously and the smaller famines that followed, political tension was increasing with anti-English feeling on the rise. Though the Troubles and the fight for Irish independence were still years away, the people of Ireland had little love for Queen Victoria or her government. That was especially true for the bailiffs who frequently evicted farmers from land they had worked on for generations after falling into debt. Independence groups such as the Fenians were already pushing for a separate Irish state and every new incident of English indifference meant change was coming. But with that need for change, many of the Irish people living in the countryside remained deeply rooted in the past. Faith in the old pagan traditions, including belief in the fairies was strong despite attempts by the Church to root it out. While the Church attempted to act as a moderating influence on the Irish people, stories of fairies still flourished and cases involving "changelings" were still being reported to the local authorities. According to folklore, changelings were the offspring of fairies or elves who were left in the place of human children abducted into fairy lands. Though belief in changelings was hardly limited to Ireland, it was still an Irish tradition that children believed to be changelings needed to be burned. Throughout the last half of the 19th century, death registries covering rural areas showed numerous entries describing "accidental" deaths of young children which the coroner rarely, if ever, questioned. Since changelings feared fire, burning was usually the last resort when other forms of exorcism were tried and failed. It was only by killing the changeling that the "true" child could be retrieved from fairy captivity. And it was not only children who were taken. Young women of childbearing age were also believed to be a favourite target for fairy abductions. Though women went missing from time to time, the possibility that they had been stolen by fairies was often raised though authorities dismissed it as local superstition. When 25-year old Bridget Cleary was reported missing in March, 1895, the exact circumstances of her disappearance seemed bizarre enough. Both she and her husband Michael were fairly well-off. Not only was Michael a cooper (barrel-maker) with a good living but Bridget was a skilled tradeswoman with her own egg business. Living in a well-kept cottage in the town of Ballyvadlea, in the heart of County Tipperary, they both seemed progressive enough except for Michael's persistent belief in fairies. That belief seemed reinforced by the location of their cottage which was very close to a rath (or ringfort) that had the reputation of being a fairy dwelling. Though Michael insisted that Bridget keep her distance from the rath, she reportedly had a fascination with the place and often visited it. According to what he told police investigating her disappearance, Bridget had been ill for several days and he had arranged for one of the local women to tend her while he was working. After Bridget went missing, the woman tending her would later insist that she had been "drawn away" and Michael would tell police that she had been taken by the fairies. The story became the talk of the countryside as police failed to turn up any trace of the missing woman. The local newspaper, the Channel Chronicle would have fun with the story which was titled, "Gone With The Fairies" when it came out on March 20. The story also became popular with Unionists who viewed it as proof of Irish superstition while Nationalists viewed it as a political disaster. Police also began investigating Michael Cleary but could find no evidence of any real problems between him and his wife. Though they were both known to have strong personalities and differences of opinion, the only remarkable thing about their marriage was their not having children after eight years together. What gave Bridget a reputation for being "a little queer" was that she seemed to enjoy her childless status (which definitely set her apart from the other country women). That, along with her fascination with Ireland's fairy lore and her tendency to look men straight in the eye, meant that she was becoming more independent than her husband found comfortable. There were even rumours that she snuck off to the ringfort to meet a lover though no real proof of this was ever found. Whatever Bridget thought about fairy lore, there was no question that Michael Cleary believed. His own mother had disappeared for a time and was rumoured to have visited the fairies and returned. That she was also named Bridget made him think that history would repeat itself with his wife. On March 6, Bridget visited the rath and returned stating that she was feeling unwell. Friends and neighbours would later report that Bridget was showing signs of "fairy-induced illness" including general aches and chills. She also had difficulty remembering familiar faces. According to Irish folklore, Bridget's symptoms suggested that she was experiencing a "fairy stroke" due to having been abducted. That she didn't seem like herself was a disturbing sign and Michael also decided that her physical appearance had changed. As he would later insist, the woman who had returned from the ringfort was two inches taller than his wife. That, combined with her general listlessness and irritability led him to conclude that she was actually a changeling who had been sent by the fairies in place of his wife. Bridget's father, aunt and cousin agreed with him and various visitors came to a similar conclusion. That Bridget might have simply been ill with bronchitis or influenza seemed not to have been considered (despite the fact that her mother had died of influenza the year before). On March 16, 1895, Michael Cleary and two family members walked two miles to the Catholic church in Drangan and spoke with the parish priest, Father M'Grath and the curate Father Ryan. All three men were in a distraught state but Michael Cleary was especially agitated. According to later reports, he began "tearing his hair and behaving like a mad man" before demanding confession. The priest refused to provide confession given Cleary's state of mind but he was able to persuade him to tell what had happened. Though Michael Cleary was largely incoherent, it was the man with him, John Dunne, who told the priests that Cleary had burned his wife to death. At that point, Michael insisted that he had not done it alone and that others had taken part in killing Bridget Cleary. Dunne, for his part, insisted that he had not taken part in the killing but wanted to arrange a Christian burial for Bridget. Little explanation was really needed by the priests since they both knew about fairy lore and the rumours that Bridget had been replaced by a changeling. Both priests had been called in several times to see Bridget during her illness and to confer the sacraments on her. There had certainly been burnings of suspected changelings before in that parish despite attempts by the Church to stamp out "pagan practices". For whatever reason, neither priest contacted authorities though Michael Cleary was escorted off the church grounds. Under Church law, anyone taking part in paganism would be denied Catholic rites. Which was definitely a blow to Michael Cleary who was obviously hoping for the Church's help in getting his real wife back from the fairies. According to Irish tradition, priests had the power to compel fairies to return abductees provided they acted in time. Instead, Father Ryan sent for a police officer to take Michael's statement. He said nothing about the confessed burning, only that Bridget Cleary was missing and that foul play was suspected. Still, Michael was furious with the priest and refused to issue any statement to the police except that his wife had disappeared. It was Constable Patrick Egan who saw Michael Cleary and John Dunne back to Ballyvadlea. Though the rumours about Bridget Cleary's apparent fairy abduction were already known by just about everyone in the area, that the "changeling" had been burned was something Michael had no interest in sharing with the police. Not that Constable Egan wasn't already aware that something had happened to make the priests turn their backs on Michael Cleary. When the cooper continued to insist that his wife had gone missing, the constable organized a police search while continuing to focus on his chief suspect. Killing the Changeling (Part 2 of 3) Continued from Part One After visiting Michael Cleary in his cottage and questioning him again about Bridget's disappearance, Constable Egan then questioned Bridget's father, Patrick Boland, who had been living with them. Patrick was extremely distraught and said nothing more than, "My daughter will come back home, my daughter will come back home." Though local police were reluctant to investigate crimes linked to fairy lore (which tended to stir up the traditional country folk), Constable Egan decided to take his investigation further. Searching the Cleary cottage while Michael was away, Egan found a half-burned nightdress and a vial of unidentified liquid. Deciding that he now had enough evidence to take to his superiors, Egan informed District Inspector Alfred Wansbrough that he suspected "foul play" in Bridget Cleary's disappearance. Wansbrough had enough experience with similar crimes and, being an English appointee, welcomed the opportunity to investigate a crime that would put the Irish people in a bad light. While the police search for Bridget Cleary was still going on, investigators also began questioning Michael Cleary and family members more closely. After being stonewalled by family members and neighbours, police finally got lucky and spoke with William Simpson and his wife, Mary. Despite being Protestant and thus out of place in the largely Catholic community, the Simpsons had been on friendly terms with the Clearys. Both Simpsons admitted visiting Bridget on the night before she allegedly ran off. In a deposition, William Simpson reported seeing Bridget subjected to a "fairy trial" which largely involved her being restrained on her bed while her husband forced her to swallow some special herbs believed to prove her changeling status. He also reported his disgust at seeing the trial but denied seeing anything else that might provide a clue to her fate. With Simpson's statement to guide them, the investigators then turned to a neighbour, Johanna Burke, who had cared for Bridget at the time of her disappearance. Though denying seeing anything wrong at first, she eventually confessed to witnessing Bridget being subjected to a fairy trial in which Michael Cleary poured urine on her and conducted an exorcism to prove her identity. Along with Michael Cleary, she implicated John Dunne and several other family members. Based on the evidence they had, police arrested Michael Cleary and all the men who were at the fairy trial. They also arrested Johanna Burke to force her to testify against the others. Along with the other men arrested, police also charged Denis Ganey, a local "fairy doctor" who had provided the herbs and other ritual cure used in Bridget's fairy trial. Though Ganey had not been present at the trial, William Simpson's statement indicated that the fairy doctor was involved to some extent. The investigation into Bridget Cleary's disappearance had a vested political element and the prosecutors hoped to focus a spotlight on popular Irish superstitions and how strong they were in the Irish countryside. Not surprisingly, the case generated considerable publicity with Nationalist and Conservative newspapers each reporting the story from their own particular viewpoint. Police were also searching the entire area for Bridget's body since they no longer believed she would be found alive. On the following day, March 22, police found evidence of disturbed soil on a spot just 1,300 yards away from the cottage. After digging, they found a narrow grave containing a body wrapped in a blanket with a bag drawn over the head. The dead female had horrible burns across her back and lower abdomen although the head and face were completely intact. While the facial features were "much distorted", it was definitely the body of Bridget Cleary. The blanket in which the body had been wrapped matched another blanket found in the Cleary cottage. The coroner's inquest was held March 23 and the jurors were given full evidence including viewing the body. Since the face was intact, the jurors could see that it was Bridget Cleary's body (many of the people present had known her all her life). The examining physicians presented their own conclusions that she had died of "shock, due to burns" and that she had either died while being burned or very shortly afterward. No other signs of violence were found on the body except for some signs suggesting that she had been restrained. The jury's verdict was that Bridget had died of burns but could not confirm how the burns had occurred. That a woman had apparently been burned to death and police arresting eleven people , including a well-known fairy doctor, made the story international news. Though cases of suspected changelings being burned had occurred in the past, the circumstances of Bridget Cleary's death focused a spotlight on Irish traditional practices as it never had before. When the Nationalist ran the story on March 23, the first printing sold out immediately and editors ordered a second edition which sold out as well. The London Times reported the story as a "shocking occurrence, recalling the barbarities practiced in the Middle Ages upon prisoners charged with witchcraft." As expected, the case quickly became political with English newspapers harping on Irish barbarity and superstition. Many of the newspapers incorrectly declared Bridget Cleary's death to be a case of "witch burning" with no attempt at explaining Irish folklore. Even court documents would label it "the Tipperary Witchcraft Case" and English newspapers used the phrase as well. In reaction to the emotionally charged atmosphere surrounding the case, local authorities imposed a news blackout which the newspapers largely respected. Then came the bizarre problem of burying Bridget's body. With her husband and most of her family in jail, there was nobody to claim the body and grant it an honourable burial. Since the Church denied the sacraments to anyone suspected of practicing fairycraft, no priest was willing to take charge either. The police solved the problem by arranging a simple wood coffin and discreetly burying Bridget's body in a local cemetery. They were careful to bury Bridget in unconsecrated ground, not far from where her mother was buried. No marker was placed on her grave, just an upturned stone. This left authorities with another problem: prosecuting the ones they believed responsible for Bridget's murder. The case continued to generate international headlines and Irish "heathen practices" were under the spotlight as they never had been before. Chief Inspector Wansbrough publicly released all details relating to Bridget Cleary's exorcism that he gathered from questioning the defendants in the case. Based on what was learned, Bridget had fallen ill on March 6 and her illness grew steadily worse over the next three days. Though they had sent for a medical doctor to tend her, it took another five days for him to arrive and he dismissed her symptoms as being a mild case of bronchitis. With no relief available from modern medicine, Michael Cleary and his family members turned to fairy lore and the belief that the real Bridget Cleary had been replaced by a changeling. According to Irish fairy lore, once someone had been abducted by fairies, family members had only nine days to retrieve him or her from the fairies. Otherwise, that person would be lost forver. Since Bridget was believed to have been abducted on March 6, that meant that Micheal had little time remaining to get her back. With only two days remaining to him, Michael purchased a remedy from a local fairy doctor. This remedy, known as the Seven Sisters cure was considered a "kill or cure" measure, only to be used in extreme cases. When the priests refused to help him, he decided to take matters into his own hands. What then followed, based on the testimony provided by Joanna Burke and others, was a long vigil while Michael Cleary and others forced Bridget to swallow the Kill or Cure herbs provided by the fairy doctor. Since Bridget refused to take the herbs insisting they were "too bitter", the men basically tried forcing the liquid down her throat. When she was unable to swallow any more (even when threatened with a red-hot poker), Michael and the others consulted Denis Ganey, the most legendary of the local fairy doctors. It was Ganey who provided the "nine-in-one" cure to the distraught husband though he never saw Bridget himself. Then came the bizarre scene which William Simpson witnessed with John Dunne, and several of Joanna Burke's brothers gathered around Bridget's bead forcing Ganey's cure down her throat. At the same time, Michael Cleary was invoking the Trinity to force the changeling to reveal herself (the task that he wanted one of the priests to perform). When she refused to respond correctly, he then threw urine on her face and chest (urine was regarded as a purifying agent). It was an exhausting ritual that took many hours. When all this failed, the men took the next step and held her over an open fire to force the changeling's cooperation. At first the men simply threatened her with the fire but eventually pushed her into the fireplace and demanded that she prove her identity. Though Bridget managed to convince the other men that she was "cured", her husband was not so easily convinced. After leaving them both to attend the funeral of Michael's father (he had decided that subjecting his wife to a fairy trial was more important than attending himself), Michael was left alone with Bridget for the first time in days.

According to fairy lore, a departing fairy was supposed to escape up a chimney and he had seen no sign of that with Bridget. On Friday morning he summoned Father Ryan to the cottage to give a mass and presumably drive the changeling out once and for all. The mass would prove controversial due to later allegations that Bridget spat out the communion wafer (which the priest denied). Johanna Burke and others would swear that Bridget spat out the wafer which, in their eyes, proved that she was a changeling. After the priest left and the men who had conducted the fairy trial continued to argue but Micheal Cleary grew increasingly desperate since the herbal brew was having no effect.

After visiting Michael Cleary in his cottage and questioning him again about Bridget's disappearance, Constable Egan then questioned Bridget's father, Patrick Boland, who had been living with them. Patrick was extremely distraught and said nothing more than, "My daughter will come back home, my daughter will come back home." Though local police were reluctant to investigate crimes linked to fairy lore (which tended to stir up the traditional country folk), Constable Egan decided to take his investigation further. Searching the Cleary cottage while Michael was away, Egan found a half-burned nightdress and a vial of unidentified liquid. Deciding that he now had enough evidence to take to his superiors, Egan informed District Inspector Alfred Wansbrough that he suspected "foul play" in Bridget Cleary's disappearance. Wansbrough had enough experience with similar crimes and, being an English appointee, welcomed the opportunity to investigate a crime that would put the Irish people in a bad light. While the police search for Bridget Cleary was still going on, investigators also began questioning Michael Cleary and family members more closely. After being stonewalled by family members and neighbours, police finally got lucky and spoke with William Simpson and his wife, Mary. Despite being Protestant and thus out of place in the largely Catholic community, the Simpsons had been on friendly terms with the Clearys. Both Simpsons admitted visiting Bridget on the night before she allegedly ran off. In a deposition, William Simpson reported seeing Bridget subjected to a "fairy trial" which largely involved her being restrained on her bed while her husband forced her to swallow some special herbs believed to prove her changeling status. He also reported his disgust at seeing the trial but denied seeing anything else that might provide a clue to her fate. With Simpson's statement to guide them, the investigators then turned to a neighbour, Johanna Burke, who had cared for Bridget at the time of her disappearance. Though denying seeing anything wrong at first, she eventually confessed to witnessing Bridget being subjected to a fairy trial in which Michael Cleary poured urine on her and conducted an exorcism to prove her identity. Along with Michael Cleary, she implicated John Dunne and several other family members. Based on the evidence they had, police arrested Michael Cleary and all the men who were at the fairy trial. They also arrested Johanna Burke to force her to testify against the others. Along with the other men arrested, police also charged Denis Ganey, a local "fairy doctor" who had provided the herbs and other ritual cure used in Bridget's fairy trial. Though Ganey had not been present at the trial, William Simpson's statement indicated that the fairy doctor was involved to some extent. The investigation into Bridget Cleary's disappearance had a vested political element and the prosecutors hoped to focus a spotlight on popular Irish superstitions and how strong they were in the Irish countryside. Not surprisingly, the case generated considerable publicity with Nationalist and Conservative newspapers each reporting the story from their own particular viewpoint. Police were also searching the entire area for Bridget's body since they no longer believed she would be found alive. On the following day, March 22, police found evidence of disturbed soil on a spot just 1,300 yards away from the cottage. After digging, they found a narrow grave containing a body wrapped in a blanket with a bag drawn over the head. The dead female had horrible burns across her back and lower abdomen although the head and face were completely intact. While the facial features were "much distorted", it was definitely the body of Bridget Cleary. The blanket in which the body had been wrapped matched another blanket found in the Cleary cottage. The coroner's inquest was held March 23 and the jurors were given full evidence including viewing the body. Since the face was intact, the jurors could see that it was Bridget Cleary's body (many of the people present had known her all her life). The examining physicians presented their own conclusions that she had died of "shock, due to burns" and that she had either died while being burned or very shortly afterward. No other signs of violence were found on the body except for some signs suggesting that she had been restrained. The jury's verdict was that Bridget had died of burns but could not confirm how the burns had occurred. That a woman had apparently been burned to death and police arresting eleven people , including a well-known fairy doctor, made the story international news. Though cases of suspected changelings being burned had occurred in the past, the circumstances of Bridget Cleary's death focused a spotlight on Irish traditional practices as it never had before. When the Nationalist ran the story on March 23, the first printing sold out immediately and editors ordered a second edition which sold out as well. The London Times reported the story as a "shocking occurrence, recalling the barbarities practiced in the Middle Ages upon prisoners charged with witchcraft." As expected, the case quickly became political with English newspapers harping on Irish barbarity and superstition. Many of the newspapers incorrectly declared Bridget Cleary's death to be a case of "witch burning" with no attempt at explaining Irish folklore. Even court documents would label it "the Tipperary Witchcraft Case" and English newspapers used the phrase as well. In reaction to the emotionally charged atmosphere surrounding the case, local authorities imposed a news blackout which the newspapers largely respected. Then came the bizarre problem of burying Bridget's body. With her husband and most of her family in jail, there was nobody to claim the body and grant it an honourable burial. Since the Church denied the sacraments to anyone suspected of practicing fairycraft, no priest was willing to take charge either. The police solved the problem by arranging a simple wood coffin and discreetly burying Bridget's body in a local cemetery. They were careful to bury Bridget in unconsecrated ground, not far from where her mother was buried. No marker was placed on her grave, just an upturned stone. This left authorities with another problem: prosecuting the ones they believed responsible for Bridget's murder. The case continued to generate international headlines and Irish "heathen practices" were under the spotlight as they never had been before. Chief Inspector Wansbrough publicly released all details relating to Bridget Cleary's exorcism that he gathered from questioning the defendants in the case. Based on what was learned, Bridget had fallen ill on March 6 and her illness grew steadily worse over the next three days. Though they had sent for a medical doctor to tend her, it took another five days for him to arrive and he dismissed her symptoms as being a mild case of bronchitis. With no relief available from modern medicine, Michael Cleary and his family members turned to fairy lore and the belief that the real Bridget Cleary had been replaced by a changeling

Though the priest would deny it, Joanna Burke and others would swear that Bridget spat out the wafer which proved that she was a changeling. After the priest left and the men who had conducted the fairy trial continued to argue whether Bridget was a changeling. Micheal Cleary grew increasingly desperate since the nine days were almost up. As midnight approached on March 15, he decided to resume the fairy trial and, when she failed to respond as he believed his real wife would, became physically abusive. After throwing her to the ground, he tried to force bread down Bridget's throat. That there were three grown men watching this ordeal along with Joanna Burke who did nothing to defend Bridget Cleary would be used against them in the later trial. Realizing that she was unresponsive, and likely dead by that time, Michael Cleary then grabbed a can of oil and poured its contents on Bridget's body before setting it on fire. Despite efforts by Joanna Burke to stop the burning, she was pushed aside. None of the others made any effort to stop Michael and Bridget was apparently already dead given that she failed to react to the burning. Though several of the others tried to leave, Michael had locked the cottage to prevent the fairy from escaping. He insisted that the body he was burning was not his wife and nobody tried to overpower him despite the body burning for more than thirty minutes. After the flames died down, Michael had the men help him lift Bridget's body onto the fireplace. After thirty more minutes, the people present watched Bridget's body burn and nobody attempted to leave despite the smoke. As the body burned, Michael Cleary kept up the ritual to drive the changeling away. After the body cooled, the men wrapped the charred body in a bedsheet to be buried by Michael Cleary and one of the other men. They then established the cover story that Bridget had "run off" and all the ones present, including Joanna Burke and Bridget's father, were made to swear oaths not to reveal what had happened. Afterward, John Dunne (who had not been present at the burning) convinced Michael to go to the priests and request their help. When the priests refused, Michael and a large group of Bridget's friends and family went to the ringfort in an attempt to get the "real" Bridget back. Michael refused to admit that he had killed his wife (who he still insisted was a changeling) and insisted that Bridget would be there according to fairy lore. Despite several long vigils, no sign of Bridget or the fairies were ever found. All that was left to them was a body that the police would later find and the later arrest of ten men for Bridget's brutal death. The arraignment of the ten men involved in the "Tipperary Witchcraft case" became major news across the United Kingdom, both for the lurid details of Bridget's murder and as an indictment of Irish fairy lore. Autopsy results showed that Bridget Cleary had been burned to death and doctors ruled out the possibility that the fairy herbs she had been forced to consume might have played a role. That exonerated Denis Ganey who had supplied the remedy that Michael had given Bridget. The others were not so fortunate. After less than an hour of deliberation, the magistrates ruled that all nine men were liable in Bridget Cleary's death and bound all of them over for a later trial. Awaiting trial, the nine men were held at the Clonmel gaol where they faced an odd predicament. Despite their numerous ties to the community, they were also regarded with some contempt for the disgrace they had brought to the entire area. Held over until July 1895, the men finally went on trial for Bridget Cleary's murder. As expected, the British government used the trial as an opportunity to not only prosecute the men but to serve as a general indictment of Irish superstition and the Catholic Church as well. Michael Cleary refused to plead guilty for his wife' murder and the jury returned a verdict of manslaughter in his case. As for the others, eight were found guilty as charged (one was acquitted because of his youth). They were given varied sentences ranging from five years to six months hard labour. Mary Kennedy, the only woman among the defendants and the mother of Joanna Burke, was allowed to go free. As for Michael Cleary, who was judged to have the primary reponsibility for his wife's murder, he was sentenced to twenty years in prison. The community reaction to the sentencing was muted but someone obviously felt outraged. Not long afterward, Mary Kennedy's cottage was burned although the Cleary cottage was left untouched. Media reaction to the sentencing fell along predictable political lines with defenders insisting that Michael Cleary's sentence was too harsh (since he genuinely believed his wife had been replaced by a changeling) to others insisting that Michael Cleary's sentence needed to stand as an example for other people contemplating "witch burning." William Simpson was reprimanded for operating paid tours of the Cleary cottage (he had been entrusted with a key which was promptly taken away from him). Rumours that the Madame Tussaud Museum in London was planning to buy the cottage never panned out either. For the most part, the people of Clonmel hoped that the entire matter would be forgotten and they largely got their wish. Michael Cleary served fifteen years of his twenty-year sentence in three different prisons before being released on parole in 1910. Part of the basis for that parole was his admitting that he had changed his mind about fairies and changelings. In his repeated parole applications, he placed most of the blame on his relatives for convincing him that his wife

was a changeling and that he was a victim of their "superstition of sorcery."
He also blamed the murder on his poor mental state stemming from his
lack of sleep while caring for his ailing wife. After his release, he never
returned to Ireland but instead emigrated to Montreal, Quebec. What
happened to him afterward appears lost to history. As for the others
prosecuted for Bridget Cleary's murder, they all served their full sentence
but many of them were left homeless following their release from prison.
Even Joanna Burke suffered considerably in the years following the trial
since many family members condemned her for testifying for the
prosecution. While the murder of Bridget Cleary was prime political fodder
at the time, there seems to be little evidence that it had much of an effect
on delaying Home Rule in Ireland. It was the only "fairy killing" of its kind to
gain international publicity but, ironically enough, a similar case occurred
only a year after Bridget Cleary's death. In a town in western Ireland, a
shoemaker named James Cunningham was bludgeoned to death by family
members after he reportedly attacked his father claiming that there were
"fairies at his throat." According to the subsequent police investigation,
James had also been in the habit of visiting a nearby fairy fort and
developed "evidence of mental affliction." Though his family attempted to
have the priests provide last rites due to James' illness, the priest refused
and the family believed that he had been touched by evil spirits. After
James' bloody death, a number of people were taken into custody including
James' father, three brothers, a sister, and several neighbours (who had
burst into the house during James rampage and had helped subdue him).
While the family members were held in the local jail, they became
convinced that evil spirits had followed them and that another Cunningham
brother, Patrick, had also become possessed. The five men in the cell broke

out and attacked the six policemen on duty before being restrained. But that wasn't all. While held in another jail awaiting trial, the entire family became involved in a violent brawl. That included James' sister, Lizzie, who attacked her father trying to "draw the fairies out of his throat." While Patrick Cunningham was acquitted, two other Cunningham brothers and Lizzie were committed to asylums. From that point on, cases of "fairy possession" were treated as signs of mental illness. Though that was the last real "fairy" trial in Ireland, fairy lore continued to be part of Irish culture but pagan practices larely faded as the Catholic Church's hold became stronger and people turned to more political matters. Despite occasional lip service to the old fairy practices, hardly anyone in Ireland would publicly admit to believing in them by the dawn of the 20th century. The only surviving physical evidence of Bridget Cleary's life and death are the parish records, her unmarked grave, and the abandoned cottage where she had lived with her husband. While reports indicate that is was still standing as recently as 2000, I could find no further mention after that. Whatever fascination Bridget Cleary had for the long abandoned ring fort near her home, she eventually paid for it with her life. That her murder trial would generate international news would likely not have given her much comfort.